J. B. Priestley

An Inspe

Teacher's Guide
by Hansjörg Meyer

Ernst Klett Verlag

Stuttgart München Düsseldorf Leipzig

An Inspector Calls – Teacher's Guide
Herausgegeben von Dr. Hansjörg Meyer, Freiberg am Neckar.

Dieses Werk folgt im Deutschen der reformierten Rechtschreibung und Zeichensetzung.

1. Auflage   1 ⁵ ⁴ ³ ² ¹ | 2000 99 98 97 96

Die letzte Zahl bezeichnet das Jahr dieses Druckes.
© Ernst Klett Verlag GmbH, Stuttgart 1996.
Alle Rechte vorbehalten.

Redaktion: Helen Smyth.

Umschlagfoto: McCabe's, London.
Druck: W. Röck, Weinsberg.
Printed in Germany.
ISBN 3-12-575211-6

Gedruckt auf Recyclingpapier,
hergestellt aus 100 % Altpapier.

Contents

Introduction

Play-reading is still one of the most enjoyable literary classroom activities, even in the media age. It is always amazing how a scene read in class, however badly, brings out the dramatic qualities of a play and naturally provokes discussion of the characters' behaviour and problems. This is particularly true of more conventional plays which are realistic in the general sense of the word, particularly if the subject matter is contemporary and close to the readers' everyday lives. In this case, it is not difficult to make pupils accept a play as being immediately relevant to themselves, rather than a painful exercise with remote literature whose importance they often only grudgingly accept because it is part of the curriculum.

From that point of view, Priestley's *An Inspector Calls* is very suitable for class work. Of course, one could argue that the literary merit of the play is controversial, and that the pupils should get to know the great writers. This is partly true, but then Priestley is one of the most popular British writers of this century, and his plays are very typical of mainstream British drama. Most British theatregoers would, at the very least have heard of *An Inspector Calls*, even if they associate it with school performances and even if amateur performances all over the world have just about ruined the play and almost removed it from the realms of "literature".

The question of literary value is tricky, as is the critical and popular esteem of writers. In fact, the latter has changed most surprisingly; many Nobel Prize winners for literature are now completely forgotten. It is true that Priestley has always been neglected by the "serious" critics as too conventional and just not modern enough, but his neglect by the guardians of literary taste possibly has more to do with a phenomenon which is normally far more pronounced in the literary scene in Germany than in Britain, namely that writers stand a fair chance of being considered good if nobody reads them and the critics praise them, whereas popular writers tend to be considered bad just because they are popular. *An Inspector Calls* may not be one of the greatest plays ever written, but the 1992 production at the National Theatre, which was celebrated as a great theatre event, showed that it still has great potential. In any case, *An Inspector Calls* is extremely suitable for classroom reading: it is easily accessible, the court-room atmosphere keeps up the suspense, and above all, despite its specific English background, the play provides many starting-points for discussions about human relations, values, and generally the way we live together in our society. In other words, it lends itself to a pupil-orientated approach, i.e. teaching should not aim at a comprehensive, academically correct interpretation of the play, but at getting the pupils to discuss points and topics they can relate to, at helping them to find out that literature can be meaningful and can help us to understand our society better.

Left to their own devices, pupils often come up with surprising aspects, which, while they may not be very relevant academically, are important for them personally. Pupils get easily frustrated if they are forced into following standard classroom approaches aimed at producing academically correct arguments. This *Teacher's Guide* therefore pursues the following line: the pupils should work closely with the text, but they should be allowed to articulate their views and opinions, even if their contributions to the discussion apparently "sidetrack" the general approach.

The language of the play encourages a pupil-orientated approach: aided by the annotations, pupils are usually able to read and understand the play very quickly. In my experience, they want to finish it once they have started reading: the suspense created by the "whodunit" structure and the increasing complexity of the plot ensure this. As language is not usually much of a barrier when doing this play, the pupils gain confidence early on and learn that they are able to discuss literature in the foreign language.

The Additional Texts have been chosen especially to develop certain themes in *An Inspector Calls*. These can be used whenever the need arises, e.g. text 5. "The Labour Market" (**96–97**) relates to Birling's dismissal of Eva Smith; text 9. "The Many Aspects of Charity" (**101–102**) develops the theme of Mrs Birling and her charity work. The texts may be referred to in the course of reading the play or at the end as a way of repeating and possibly clarifying particular points.

How to Use this *Guide*

The *Teacher's Guide* provides a detailed lesson-to-lesson plan complete with homework assignments. The lessons may be used in a different sequence to the one given here, particularly after the first few lessons when the play as a whole comes into perspective.

The *Questions* (pp. 10–17) facilitate a more flexible approach. The three sets of questions are numbered continuously for easy reference and can be copied and used as worksheets.

1) *Quiz Questions*
   These can be done individually for fun, or for homework, or they can be referred to when convenient.

2) *Comprehension Questions*
   Arranged according to acts, these questions can be given as homework, either before or after the relevant parts of the play have been discussed. These questions are often based on quotes or refer to small details to make them easier to cope with, but like the pieces in a puzzle, the corresponding answers help to form a more general picture.

3) *Integrated Questions*
   These refer to the play as a whole or suggest classic essay topics.

The length of the list of questions not only means that pupils have a choice but also the teacher can put together an individual selection of questions for each classes' needs and interests. Specific questions are suggested for each lesson and these often provide relevant vocabulary and phrases for pupils to articulate their ideas. The comprehension questions, in particular, are meant to provide a sort of running commentary, thus pointing out certain aspects and suggesting possible approaches.

Pre-reading Activities

An important phase of a pupil-orientated approach to literature involves the completion of pre-reading activities. These help pupils to think along particular lines before they read the text. The more extensive and intensive the pre-reading activities are, the easier it is for the pupils to approach the text. Ideally, the play, should not seem to be separate from reality, i.e. just "literature", but a literary text using the stage as a forum. (see point 4, p. 10)

The following pre-reading activities for *An Inspector Calls* introduce questions of crime and guilt, good and evil, right and wrong, and society's methods of dealing with these.

1) Pupils should consider the following questions about law and morality. These have been broken down under three headings:

Personal Experiences:
Have you ever been involved in police proceedings?
Have you ever been questioned, e.g. as a witness?
Describe your experiences.

Crime:
Have there been any spectacular crimes in your home town recently? (corruption, tax evasion, labour troubles, divorce cases, etc.)
How did the general public react? Was there a consensus?
How did the press react?
What did you feel?

Law Enforcement:
What is the role of the police and of legal institutions?
Can they deal with everything that is considered wrong in society?
Which moral standards can law courts enforce, which can they not enforce?

2) The next step could be to discuss Belloc's *The Justice of the Peace*, which satirizes an extreme example of how these problems are worked out in a certain type of society.

Starting Question: What is the function of a judge?

When a crime has been committed, the police initiates inquiries, and if those involved are caught, the case is normally presented in court by a prosecutor. All defendants are to be treated equally in the eyes of the law, i.e. the defendant's financial or social situation do not matter. Judges are required to have a degree in law so that they are competent enough to decide independently. They must also be absolutely neutral and to ensure this, they are paid a salary (in Germany, they are civil servants). In comparison, justices of the peace in Britain are unpaid and usually have no legal training. They are respected citizens who have the authority to deal with minor cases and many justices do a lot of valuable work in the community.

Belloc's satirical poem however exposes the potential weaknesses of this legal institution. His justice of the peace cannot be neutral as he has his own interests to protect. He sees his job as a means of keeping society as it is, i.e. as an unjust class society. "Obeying" the law means the law as he interprets it, as a landowner and "Lord benign".

The key to the poem is line 8: "because I have" which could be paraphrased as: "Because I am a landowner, I am a justice of the peace and have the upper hand. If you remember your low status, nothing will happen to you." Here, justice is seen almost as a charity, and not as a human right. It is the same unholy alliance of property, power, class and law that Birling tries to intimidate the Inspector with, in Priestley's play. Pupils can return to the poem later to consider what sort of justice of the peace Birling is.

3) After the class has been generally introduced to the subject matter of the play and has become familiar with some of the relevant vocabulary, pupils can move towards literature proper.

Starting Question: Do you know any plays about crime and criminals, justice, guilt, etc.?

As pupils will probably first refer to TV thrillers, they could answer some of the following questions:

What do the plots of thrillers and crime stories often concentrate on?
How do these thrillers affect the audience/you?

What do they tell us about crime and criminals in our society?
Can you think of a play that really made you think?

References could be made to some good TV thrillers, as well as to, e.g. *Die Räuber, Woyzeck,* some Hauptmann plays, Wedekind's *Frühlings Erwachen* or similar works. The most important criterion for this activity is that the discussion moves beyond the "whodunit" aspect of the problems of crime and society, justice and morality.

4) In order to get a discussion going, pupils could look at Additional Text: 14. "The Theatre as a Political Forum" by John McGrath (**110**), if it was not used at the beginning of this pre-reading phase. (see Working with the Additional Texts p. 48–49)

5) Finally, there could be a short brainstorming session on the title of the play: *An Inspector Calls.*

Questions:
What does the title mean?
What does it lead you to expect?
Is the Inspector expected or unexpected?
How would people react in such a case? How would you react?
What does the title imply the play could be about?

Questions

Quiz

How well do you know the text? Place the following quotations in their dramatic context, i.e. say what happened before this; why the character says this; how the other characters react, etc.

Act I

1) You seem to be a nice well-behaved family.
2) Sounds a bit fishy to me.
3) Here, what do you mean?
4) It's the way I like to go to work.
5) ... there's nothing mysterious – or scandalous – about this business ...

6) A chain of events.
7) I don't like the tone.
8) I'd have let her stay.
9) But these girls aren't cheap labour – they're people.
10) And I think you'd better stay here.
11) So I'm really responsible?
12) Yes, but you can't. It's too late. She's dead.
13) We can't leave it at that.
14) Yes. We can keep it from him.

Act II

15) Why should you? It's bound to be unpleasant and disturbing.
16) You see, we have to share something.
17) But it's you – and not the Inspector here – who's doing it –
18) He must wait his turn.
19) Well, we didn't think you meant Buckingham Palace.
20) I must say, we are learning something tonight.
21) Yes, but why are you saying that to him? You ought to be saying it to me.
22) Your daughter isn't living on the moon. She's here in Brumley too.
23) Look here, this wasn't Gerald Croft –
24) A lot of nonsense – I didn't believe a word of it.
25) Who is to blame then?
26) Not yet. I'm waiting.

Act III

27) If you'd had any sense of loyalty –
28) I don't want any of that talk from you –
29) You don't understand anything.
30) Don't talk rubbish. Of course it does.
31) He was our police inspector all right.
32) Well, I didn't notice you standing up to him.
33) Now – now – we needn't bother him with all that stuff.
34) I suppose we're all nice people now.
35) I wish I'd been here when that man first arrived.
36) Now it's our turn.

37) According to you, I ought to feel a lot better.
38) No, he didn't. And I see what you mean now.
39) It will look a bit queer, won't it – ringing up at this time of night. –
40) Well, why shouldn't we?

Comprehension Questions

Act I

1) Mrs Birling is "her husband's social superior" (**6** 5). How is this shown in the opening scene?
2) Sum up the situation and atmosphere in the dining-room before the Inspector's arrival.
3) How does Birling see the engagement between Sheila and Gerald?
4) Why does Birling mention his knighthood to Gerald, even though it is still uncertain?
5) Why does Birling mention his official functions and his connections to the Inspector? Discuss how he deals with the Inspector throughout this scene.
6) Why does Gerald want to be "out of this" (**20** 11–12)?
7) Describe Eric's behaviour in the opening scene and after the Inspector has arrived.
8) Why exactly did Birling sack Eva? How do the others react to this?
9) "It's about time you learnt to face a few responsibilities" (**23** 31–32). What exactly does Birling mean when he says this to Eric?
10) "I don't play golf" (**23** 19). What does this statement by the Inspector imply in the context of this scene?
11) Why does the Inspector not show the photograph to everyone at the same time?
12) Why does Sheila run out after she has seen the photograph? Why does she come back shortly afterwards?
13) Why does Birling want "a word" with his wife to "tell her what's happening" (**29** 22)?
14) From a dramatic point of view, why is the Inspector made to leave before the end of Act I?
15) Sum up the dramatic situation at the end of Act I. Who knows what? How is the suspense kept up?

Act II

16) What does the Inspector's introductory "Well?" (**36** 6) imply for the characters and for the audience?
17) Why does Sheila take such an active interest in the investigations at the beginning of Act II? Why does Gerald want her to leave? Why does she give her engagement ring back?
18) "Your daughter isn't living on the moon" (**48** 15–16). How do the others see and treat Sheila? What is she really like?
19) "I feel you're beginning all wrong" (**39** 6). Sheila says to her mother after the latter has entered the scene. Compare Mrs Birling's manner at this point, to her husband's in Act I. How do you think the audience might react to her?
20) Why is there "an exclamation of surprise from Birling and Mrs Birling" (**43** 18) when the Inspector starts questioning Gerald?
21) How is "disgusting" (e.g. **45** 14, **48** 37) used as a key word?
22) Why does Gerald want to be "alone for little while" (**50** 20) after he has been questioned by the Inspector?
23) Discuss the communication problems in the scene before Mrs Birling is questioned, e.g. "Does that mean anything, Sheila?" (**52** 20).
24) How does Mrs Birling see her own role in the victim's fate? Compare her attitude to Sheila's and Gerald's.
25) Why is Mrs Birling so angry about Eva calling herself Mrs Birling? How does this link up with her whole attitude towards "Girls of that class" (**39** 31)?
26) What strategy does Mrs Birling adopt in her interview with the Inspector?
27) What is Birling's reaction when his wife's role in the affair becomes clear?
28) Describe Birling's and Mrs Birling's emotional state at the end of Act II.
29) How do the characters develop and reveal themselves throughout Act II?
30) What is the situation at the end of Act II? What do the characters know, hope and fear? Is there still any suspense?

Act III

31) How does Eric feel about his role in the affair?
32) Describe the father-son relationship between Birling and Eric.
33) Why does the Inspector play a decreasingly active role in the course of Act III?
34) "Look, Inspector – I'd give thousands – yes, thousands –" (**69** 4–5) Birling says to the Inspector "unhappily". Why would he give so much money and to whom? What is Birling's chief worry?
35) Compare the Birlings as a family in Act III, up to the Inspector's departure and afterwards.
36) Which two main points cause disagreement in the family in Act III?
37) Discuss the different uses and meanings of "childish" (**72** 9).
38) How does Birling's and Mrs Birling's manner change after the Inspector has left, particularly after Gerald's return?
39) Why does Birling keep the newly-emerged facts from Gerald?
40) How do the Birlings and Gerald find out that Goole is not a real police inspector? Describe the process from suspicion to certainty.
41) How do the different characters react when it becomes clear that Goole was not a genuine policeman?
42) "I couldn't imagine a real police inspector talking like that to us" (**76** 8–10). Do you think Mrs Birling is right?
43) Why is Mrs Birling "most grateful" (**85** 17) to Gerald?
44) Compare the Birlings at the end of Act III with the characters we meet in the opening scene of Act I.
45) Comment on the characters' reaction to the final phone call.

Essay Topics

Dramatic Techniques/Plot

46) Is *An Inspector Calls* a thriller?
47) Why is Mrs Birling not on stage when Sheila and Birling are being questioned? Using this as a starting point, say how the plot justifies the characters' entrances and exits.
48) Discuss how Priestley's use of dramatic irony influences the audience's attitudes. Give examples.
49) The Inspector sometimes addresses the audience directly. At which points in the play does this occur and what is the intended effect?

50) Discuss the different forms of suspense in the play.
51) The telephone call at the end of the play, announcing a genuine inspector, has often been criticized. Do you think this is important for the play? Why?
52) Do you find the plot realistic or contrived?
53) The Inspector says the "young ones" are "more impressionable" (**39** 16–17). Does the play bear this out? Do you think this is generally true?
54) "If you'd had any sense of loyalty – " (**63** 2). Is Sheila being disloyal? Discuss Birling's accusation in the context of the play.
55) In the course of the play, each character becomes the centre of interest while he or she is being interrogated.
a) How do they react? Are they cooperative or uncooperative? In what way does the inquiry become a process of self-discovery?
b) Discuss how Priestley varies the underlying pattern of a police inquiry with each character.
56) Why does Priestley give such detailed stage directions?
57) What is the effect of ignoring Priestley's stage directions, e.g. the 1992 London production (see Additional Text 13)? Is it legitimate for a producer to do this?

Characters: Emotion vs. Restraint

58) Does the Inspector show emotion at any point in the play? Give examples, if any.
59) To what extent are the characters conditioned by their up-bringing and by their place in society? Are they responsible for their actions? Could they have acted differently?
60) "Not a single human relationship in the play is intact." Discuss.
61) Which of the characters most engages your sympathy, and why?
62) Real self and social role – which characters act as humans beings and which keep to their official/social roles?
63) Which of the characters changes most in the course of the play? In which cases, if any, are these changes long-term?

Inspector Goole

64) How does the fact that Goole is an outsider affect the plot?
65) In what way is the Inspector different from a genuine policeman?
66) Do you think that the fact that the Inspector is not a genuine police officer affects the message of the play?
67) Audiences all over the world have wondered what exactly Inspector Goole is and what he stands for. What do you think?
68) Discuss the Inspector's methods of inquiry.

Sheila

69) How does Sheila's and Gerald's relationship change in the play?
70) "It is very easy for Sheila and Eric to moralize over and criticize their parents because they can take their own privileged way of life for granted." Do you agree?

Eva

71) "Eva Smith is used as a foil to the other characters." Discuss.
72) Eva Smith does not appear on the stage although she holds the plot together. What kind of person does she seem to have been?
73) Why does Mrs Birling despise Eva? In her view, how should Eva have behaved to qualify as a "deserving case"?
74) What did Eva mean to Gerald and Eric, what did they mean to her? How do the two men talk about their affairs with her?

Family: The Birlings – Pretensions and Realities.

75) Show how the investigation into Eva's death gradually reveals the truth about the family.
76) The family harmony of the opening scene turns into infighting and violent quarrels. Discuss the important stages in this development.

Language

77) Describe the type of language used by the different characters.
78) Mrs Birling often censors the language used by the other characters. Find examples of this and analyse them in their context. Why does she do this? What does language mean for her?

79) Some characters talk about people outside their social circle in a way that can be characterized as "Them and Us". Discuss how this affects the characters' attitudes and the course of the play.

80) Appearances seem to be all important in this society and the truth has to be covered up by hypocrisy, pretensions, snobbery and lies. Find examples of where this happens.

Social Lie

81) The notion of keeping up appearances, as characterized in Ibsen's plays by the "social lie" *Lebenslüge*, is exposed in the Birling family. Find examples of this and discuss how this social lie affects the characters' actions.

82) Can the Titanic, mentioned by Birling in his after-dinner speech, be seen as a metaphor for the whole play?

Guilt

83) The Inspector often makes moral judgements. What are his standards and where do they come from?

84) At the end, all of the characters are guilty of Eva Smith's death. How would you differentiate in their measure of guilt?

Private and Public Morality

85) Examine the following quotes (**30** 29–33) from *An Inspector Calls* and discuss the Inspector's statement in particular in the context of the play.

"Gerald: After all, y'know, we're respectable citizens and not criminals."

Inspector: "Sometimes there isn't as much difference as you think. Often, if it was left to me, I wouldn't know where to draw the line."

86) Is *An Inspector Calls* a play of social criticism?

87) Is *An Inspector Calls* only a play about Edwardian Britain?

88) Why, do you think, has the play had such a triumphant revival in Britain and on Broadway since 1992?

The Opening Scene

The first few lessons should follow the plot and concentrate on close reading so that pupils get used to standard approaches aiming at aspects such as characterization, motivation, plot, etc.

1) The elaborate stage directions (**5** 1–**6** 14) at the beginning of the play place the Birlings socially: "prosperous", "good", "solid", "substantial" (**5** 2–4) are key words. The fact that the room is "heavily comfortable, but not cosy and homelike" (**5** 4–5) shows that it complies with class standards, i.e. it is what an upper-class dining-room is supposed to look like, not the result of personal taste.

2) Other aspects of upper-class life also become apparent at the beginning of the play: the domestic staff (cook, maid), and a formal dinner ("correct" drinks, cigars) with formal clothes, even more so than the occasion demands.
   The opening scene shows the Birlings toasting Sheila's engagement to Gerald, son of a socially superior family which signifies both a social and business success for the family.

3) Even at this stage, family harmony seems slightly threatened and the author uses various "pointers" to hint at potential problems:
   a) Eric seems different from the rest of the family – he behaves oddly as he "suddenly guffaws" (**8** 6), he speaks more directly than the others, he does not want to hear his father's toast and he seems to have a drink problem.
   b) Gerald neglected Sheila, "all last summer when you never came near me" (**7** 22–23) and she is not convinced by his excuses that he was "awfully busy" (**7** 25).
   c) Mrs Birling shows that she is "her husband's social superior" (**6** 5).
   d) Birling feels socially inferior to the Crofts, a fact which becomes explicit when he and Gerald are left alone. His mention of a *possible* knighthood is a kind of social justification.
   e) At the same time, however, he feels safe enough to joke about possible obstacles to his knighthood – in retrospect, another indication of events to come.

4) In his big speech, Birling holds forth on life and politics. As a "hard-headed, practical man of business" (**11** 34–**12** 1) the key words in-

clude "experience", "the interest of Capital", "we know", "progress", "making headway", "optimism", "a man has to make his own way". The spirit of his speech is symbolized by the "absolutely unsinkable" Titanic (**12** 13). The obstacles to progress are "these Bernard Shaws and H. G. Wellses" (**13** 1–2), and people who believe in "community and all that nonsense" (**16** 3). They are "scaremongers" (**12** 16) who are simply trying to cause trouble.

At this point, this is just a pompous after-dinner speech by somebody who wants to impress on others that he is not just a successful businessman but that he has views and is somebody even if Croft Ltd. is an older, more distinguished company. The speech takes on its full meaning only in the course of the play, when its social philosophy is defeated by the plot. Even at this point, the audience will recognize the false prophesies, if not the ideology, of Birling's speech.

Finding out the Truth

The following section deals with the characters in the order that they are interviewed and concludes with a detailed look at the two catalysts in the play, Eva and Inspector Goole.

Suggestions are made for homework assignments for each character and a key question is Essay Topic: 55) which can be related to each interrogation in turn. The question sheets can be completed simultaneously to build up a general picture of events. Alternatively this is an ideal opportunity for pair work as it gives pupils a chance to compare ideas before reporting back to the class. It could be left up to pupils to suggest which key speeches and scenes should be read in class.

Once pupils have dealt with Mrs Birling, they could start collecting relevant background information for the Essay Topics from class discussions, etc. and then use this to answer the questions more fully.

Birling

Homework: Comprehension Questions 5)–10), 13), and 55), which is a key question for the next few lessons.

The harmony of the family scene is only slightly affected when the Inspector is announced and Birling and Gerald keep up the joke about avoiding trouble, to show how safe they feel. In fact, this feeling of safety determines Birling's **strategy** towards the Inspector:

- Birling repeatedly tries to put the Inspector in his place by mentioning his own status and connections. The third time he does this, he even "warns" (**23** 15) the Inspector.
- Birling refuses all responsibility, repeating bits of his social philosophy "If we were all responsible for everything that happened to everybody we'd had anything to do with, it would be very awkward, wouldn't it?" (**21** 7–10).
- he justifies sacking Eva as a necessary business decision and his duty as an employer.
- he remains objective and distanced when he talks about "these people" (**23** 4) and he refuses to consider individual circumstances.

When he realizes other family members might be involved as well, Birling apologizes to the Inspector. This, and the fact that he wants to tell his wife "what's happening" (**29** 22), show his basic insecurity.

The other characters' reactions to Birling's interrogation vary greatly. The Inspector is not impressed by his talk and states the facts again and again, forcing Birling to admit them. As a businessman, Gerald has to agree with Birling's decision. Eric and Sheila however, criticize their father on human grounds, and this is the beginning of the family disagreement.

The following table shows the constellation of characters at this point:

(Blackboard summary)

Constellation of characters

Birling	Eva	Sheila
Gerald		Eric
	Inspector	
distanced, motivated by business considerations	knows the facts, provokes reactions, brushes away anything irrelevant	personal and moral standing

Sheila

Homework: Comprehension Questions 12), 55).

After the close reading of the Birling scene, pupils could work in pairs on Sheila's interrogation, using Essay Topics: 55) as a starting point. The results of the pair work can then be used by the class for a systematic comparison of Birling's and Sheila's defenses.

One difference is that whereas Birling starts from scratch with the Inspector, Sheila has already learned of her father's doings and reacted critically before she is herself questioned. Therefore she is already in an emotional state when the Inspector shows her the photograph. The interrogations can be compared using some of the following headings:

(Blackboard summary)

	Birling	**Sheila**
Motive:	profit, business decision	jealousy, "furious temper"
Result:	Eva is sacked	Eva is sacked
Attitude to Eva:	self-righteous, not responsible, sees Eva as employee, not bothered	feels guilty, responsible, sees Eva as a person, process of self-realization
Attitude to Inspector:	refuses Inspector's standards, tries to stop inquiry, wants to protect Sheila, blames Inspector for "nasty mess"	accepts his standards, helps actively with inquiry, wants to find out the truth, blames herself for the girl's fate
Emotions:	hard-headed businessman, reacts "officially"	impressionable, emotional, reacts as a fellow human being

So Sheila's interrogation is a complete contrast to the scene before, and bears out the Inspector's later statement that "the young ones are … more impressionable" (**39** 16–17).

Gerald

Homework: Quiz Questions I. Comprehension Questions 16)–18), 20)–22).

The end of Act I and beginning of Act II concentrate on Gerald and Sheila.

1) First, Gerald is forced to admit that he had an affair with Eva. He wants to keep this quiet, but Sheila has now taken on the Inspector's role and tells him that a cover-up is impossible.
2) Gerald's attempt to keep Sheila out of his inquiry and so keep his involvement in the affair to himself also fails. Sheila wins this power struggle and becomes more independent by the minute. For her, the quest for the truth is more important than his Edwardian preoccupation with protecting young ladies from the seamier side of life.
3) Gerald's interrogation is also a voyage of discovery for Sheila, and ends with her breaking off the engagement. Still, Gerald emerges quite positively from this scene, despite Mrs Birling's disturbing presence. His reaction is very personal as he is deeply moved and wants to be alone to come to terms with an experience he has just been forced to live through again.

As a result of this scene:
1. Eva's fate has become a family affair.
2. The family harmony of the opening scene is completely destroyed.

Mrs Birling

Homework: Mrs Birling: Comprehension Questions 23)–30).

The power struggle between Mrs Birling and the Inspector preceding Gerald's interrogation makes the latter's ultimate confession all the more remarkable. Because Mrs Birling has not been on stage since the Inspector's arrival, she uses the same strategy as her husband in Act I, to take control of the situation in that:
– she tries to intimidate the Inspector,
– she tells him there won't be any results.
By now however, the Inspector knows how to deal with the Birlings and with Sheila's help, he wins this power struggle, too. Mrs Birling

has to witness Gerald's interrogation before it is her own turn, a forthcoming event of which she is still unaware. Of course, she reacts quite differently from Sheila, and her attitude only aggravates the family crisis.

– She does not want to hear about Gerald's affair and tries to stop the inquiry.
– When she is forced to listen, she shows moral indignation.
– She makes a clear distinction between "Them and Us" with her reference to "Girls of that class" (**39** 31).
– Mrs Birling not only thinks that she is not involved and is above the situation, she also feels more than irritated at the intrusion.
– The auctorial comments all point to her acting out her social role: e.g. "briskly", "self-confidently" (**38** 24), "annoyed" (**40** 4), "haughtily" (**40** 11), "rebuking them" (**40** 30), etc.
– When irrefutable facts are revealed about Eric's drinking and Meggarty's double life, she is "staggered" (**41** 30), but keeps her ironic detachment: "I must say, we *are* learning something tonight" (**45** 21–22).

When it is her turn to admit her role in the affair however, she puts up a very stiff fight and starts the interrogation with a downright lie. Finally, it is Sheila who gives a summary of the bare facts and ensures that the interrogation of her own mother can continue.

Although the Inspector forces Mrs Birling to accept the facts bit by bit, and even Sheila and Birling begin to undermine her position, she sticks to her self-righteous attitude. The key words in this scene are: "justified" (**59** 17), "a girl of that sort" (**58** 28–29), "I accept no blame" (**59** 22) and "duty" (**60** 20). For this reason her interrogation is the most dramatic clash between class ideology and the bare facts. Only when it dawns on her that the scapegoat she has blamed everything on in a last desperate attempt to keep her stance, is her own son, does she break down "frightened" (**60** 35) and "agitated" (**61** 7).

This scene, the climax of the play, also brings out very clearly the contrast between "official" facts as symbolized by Mr and Mrs Birling "doing their duty" and the human aspects as when the Inspector says, "Her position now is that she lies with a burnt-out inside on a slab" (**58** 11–12).

Eric

Homework: Quiz Questions II. Comprehension Question 30).
Eric: Comprehension Questions 31)–33), 37).

At the beginning of Act III, both the characters and the audience know that Eric is involved in the affair, too. What they do not know are the exact details. When Eric confesses to having stolen money from his father's firm, thus directly endangering the family's reputation, infighting breaks out and it is the Inspector who has to bring the situation back under control. Once the facts have been established, the Inspector makes his final speech, which like Birling's speech in Act I, marks a point within the play from which events are judged. The message of the Inspector's speech is very simple:
- All people have hopes and fears, which are affected by other people's actions.
- "We are responsible for each other" (**69** 24–25).
- If we do not "learn" this, the consequences will be terrible.

This final prophesy shows the historical and contemporary aspects of the play. Whereas Birling's speech echoes Mrs Thatcher's notorious statement that there is no such thing as society, the Inspector demands solidarity. Pupils could analyse and compare the two speeches as a starting-point for the following projects:

1) *Social reality in Britain, 1912–1946–1992.*
2) *In your opinion, which of the two views of society prevails in your country? Support your view with relevant facts.*

Eva

Homework: Eva: Comprehension Questions 71)–74).

Working in pairs, pupils could summarize what they know about Eva and her function in the play and then report back to the class. The following should be included in this:

1) Although only her photograph is shown and she never appears on the stage in person, Eva holds the plot together. All the characters have known her at some time and together they have ruined her.

2) Eva may not really "exist", yet she develops into a very complex character as the play moves along.
3) Birling and Sheila treat her as an employee. For Sheila, she only becomes a person in retrospect. In contrast, Eva provides Gerald and Eric with something they do not have in their "official" relationships" (as fiancé and son), namely unconditional love and understanding.
4) In the end, Eva is the only moral person in the play. She is considerate and does not get Gerald and Eric into trouble, as she easily could have done. Nor does she give in to Mrs Birling by playing the role of a "deserving case", even though she is desperate. Instead she chooses to preserve her human dignity. Eva is an individual in a world where women, in particular, are forced into social roles (fiancée or "woman of the town"). She has all the qualities the Birlings pretend to have.
5) In the play, Eva puts each of the characters to the test, and they all fail. In the process, she unmasks their family ideology.

Working in pairs, pupils could compare the way Birling and Mrs Birling see Eva with the Eva who emerges from the play. The class could then put their results into a table like the one below:

(Blackboard summary)

Their View of Eva	Our View of Eva
"ringleader" (**22** 32)	working-class solidarity
"disgusting" (Gerald's affair) (**48** 37)	real relationship ("warm-hearted" **47** 34)
"giving herself ridiculous airs" (**58** 7–8)	consideration for Eric
"a lot of nonsense" (**58** 24)	truth
"Girls of that class" (**39** 31)	human being

Up to now, work in class will have roughly followed the plot. From this point onwards, more systematic approaches linking thematic aspects will become increasingly important. How the following chapters are used and put together will very much depend on each individual class, though they can be used in the sequence given here. Homework can be assigned from the questions provided for the different aspects. At this point, however, long-term assignments from the essay section should dominate work in class rather than lesson-to-lesson homework.

Inspector Goole

Homework:
At this point pupils can be assigned some of the integrated essay questions as well as the shorter comprehension questions.

Like Eva, the Inspector brings all of the characters and thematic aspects of the play together. He actually plays two roles: on the surface, the Inspector is investigating a case, and the other characters accept this role, until he is found to be a fake. As the play proceeds, the Inspector's second role as moral authority becomes clearer as he attacks and exposes the underlying social structures which lead to Eva's suicide. He forces the characters and the audience to accept his authority, which is based on commonly-accepted standards of human decency.

The Inspector's somewhat unconventional methods of inquiry are vital in this case. From the beginning, he brushes aside Birling's and later Mrs Birling's claims to special treatment. His job is to concentrate on the facts, and the characters are only relevant for him in the particular context of the case, not in the way they see themselves in their social roles. As an outsider, he breaks down all barriers of class pretensions and otherness, and consequently their whole way of life comes under investigation, when the Inspector exposes what in their social frame of reference is "normal", as being criminal and immoral. The Inspector wants the Birlings to face the truth he already knows.

The widening of the Inspector's inquiry from Eva's fate to an analysis of the society that caused this, is almost imperceptible, until it is made explicit in his final speech. Ultimately, the problem is not just that everybody has a skeleton in the cupboard, it goes much deeper than that into the rotten fabric of society.

Thematic Aspects

Family Breakdown

Homework: Essay Topics
Family: 54), 58), 60), 75)–77).
Appearances and realities: 80)–81)

The Inspector gradually makes the Birlings realize that they are not a "nice, well-behaved family" (**14** 15–16) and the family harmony of the opening scene is exposed as being false. The characters' individual failures are rooted in their relationships with each other – e.g. because her relationship with Gerald is not satisfactory, Sheila instinctively regards Eva as a rival, and naturally exercises her power as a high-class customer to have her sacked. Thus the inquiry into Eva's death develops into a process of self-discovery for the characters.

The basic pattern of the Inspector's investigation aims at showing the discrepancies between **appearances and realities**. In pairs, pupils could work out how the characters are perceived within the family and in their society in general (appearances) and what they are really like (realities).

(Blackboard summary)

	Appearances	**Realities**
Eric	lad, boy, child	has a drink problem
Meggarty	respected alderman	rogue, sot
Gerald	busy at the works	having an affair
Sheila	child who needs parental protection	knows about Meggarty, "women of the town" etc.
Birling	successful businessman	ruthless employer
Mrs Birling	does useful charity work	charity work governed by class prejudices

As the truth comes out the scene is increasingly dominated by infighting, finger-pointing and suppressed nastiness, and the Inspector can hardly keep the family on the line of inquiry. The characters' reactions to the Inspector alone seem to divide them into opposing camps. The younger people cooperate with the Inspector; Sheila because she is really shocked at the outcome of her actions, and Gerald and Eric because Eva really meant something to them – the problem of loyalty is very important in this context.

Birling, however, has no scruples, he would hush up anything and think it was normal. His main concern is to limit any possible damage to his reputation and public image as caused by the others' actions:

- Mrs Birling ensured that Eva's case was turned down by the board of the charity – Birling is afraid of a scandal if this is made public at the inquest.
- Eric stole money to help Eva after getting her into trouble, but his father's only worry is possible damage to the firm's reputation.
- Birling tries to explain away Gerald's betrayal of Sheila's trust. In the end Gerald is the hero and Mrs Birling even calls him "clever" because he has found out that Goole is not a real inspector.

The character who actually loses the most credibility during the inquiry is Birling. By the end of the play his position as the head of the family, which he frequently reminds others of, has been totally undermined. Pupils should follow his regression as they work through the text. Some of the points they may come up with are:

1) Birling gives the young people stupid, pompous advice in his after-dinner speech. Later, the Inspector and the younger members of the family show him how wrong he is.
2) Initially as the experienced and "hard-headed" (**11** 6–7) business man, Birling tries to deal with the Inspector on his own, a strategy which fails miserably. At the end of the play, he criticizes the others for letting the side down, in spite of the fact that their collective guilt has been proved beyond a doubt. Although Mrs Birling seems to support him, "Now just be quiet so that your father can decide what we ought to do" (**74** 21–22), she often undermines his authority by criticizing him in front of others.
3) Birling does not know much about his "children" but still thinks he has to protect them from reality. His relationship with Eric in particular, is not one of trust and understanding, as the latter says Birling is "not the kind of father a chap could go to when he's in trouble" (**67** 8–9).

4) His attempts to explain away Gerald's escapades only embarrass the young couple.
5) Birling cannot see beyond his own position and social role, which means that he does not understand anything.
6) He is totally class-ridden, as shown by his subservient behaviour towards Gerald. For Birling, money, power, status, justice, and morality are all the same, just like in Belloc's *The Justice of the Peace*.

Of all of the characters, Mrs Birling is the most uncompromising, even more so than her husband. She totally refuses to take responsibility for her actions. Instead she stays on her high horse of self-righteousness, working herself into a state of classical hubris and demanding exemplary punishment for the young man who got Eva into trouble and deserted her. She can do this because she is absolutely convinced that people of better class are also morally superior, i.e. that the culprit must be one of "them". Ultimately Mrs Birling only breaks down when she is forced to realize that there is no basic difference between "Them and Us" (Essay Topic: 79), between "Girls of that class" and her own children. This concept of "Them and Us", which assumes that the higher the class one is in, the higher the moral standing and worthiness of the individual, comes up again and again in the play, both implicitly and explicitly.

Not only does the family go to pieces but even their home loses some of its solidity. In the beginning, the Birling dining-room fills the whole stage and the only outward links are the doorbell, the Inspector, the photo of Eva and the telephone. Gradually, the outside world makes itself felt in this self-contained little world. Gerald and Eric go to the Palace Bar quite naturally and they meet a lot of "respectable" people there. This is another world, where the "women of the town" (44 15) are exploited by those who have made them victims of the system in the first place, as shown by the example of Eva Smith/Daisy Renton. Everybody knows about these places, but they are not mentioned officially – a good example of the double morality prevalent in Victorian and Edwardian Britain.

Appearances and Realities — A Structural Overview

Acts	I			
Scenes	**1 – 3**	**4**	**5 – 7**	**8**
develop-ments	Engagement party, family harmony, optimism, Birling's speech	Inspector arrives, Birling's interrog-ation	Sheila's interrog-ation	Sheila and Gerald disagree
Appear-ances				
Realities				

II		III		
9 – 11	12 –13	14 – 16	17	18
Gerald's interrogation, Sheila gives ring back	Mrs Birling is exposed, her hubris, climax	Eric's confession, family infighting	Parents resume authority, generation gap, suspicions about Inspector	Gerald returns, Inspector a fake, attempts to reconstruct family harmony, phone call

A Class Society

Homework: Essay Topics
Justice and Morality: 83)–86)
Language: 42), 78), 79)

By insisting on the existence of social differences, the characters show how class-conscious they really are. A variety of details ranging from the initial situation and the characters' behaviour, to small yet telling indicators like their clothes, the presence of domestic staff, and even their correct manners (dinner, correctly followed by port and cigars), etc., show that they fill certain roles in the community:

- Birling, apart from owning a factory, holds public office.
- Mrs Birling is engaged in charity work (which is about all upper-class ladies could do at that time).
- Sheila does not work, of course, but is enjoying herself preparing for her forthcoming wedding.
- Gerald is Sir George Croft's son, which is how Birling introduces him to the Inspector, and not "just" as Sheila's fiancé.

The family is part of the Establishment, and outsiders who do not know this must be told, so that they know how to behave. That is why Birling tells the Inspector all about himself and his connections. Eva however, deliberately or otherwise, broke the rules by adopting the name Birling, thus rejecting the barriers between "Them and Us".

Mrs Birling strongly believes in this difference, an attitude which obviously determines how she conducts her **charity** work. Instead of being motivated by compassion and the wish to help those in need, she wants to demonstrate her moral superiority by giving handouts. The "deserving cases" are those girls who eat humble pie and accept their lowly position as God-given. People like Eva who rebel, have to be taught a lesson.

The whole ideology of Victorian-Edwardian charity was discussed critically even before Shaw, e.g. by Oscar Wilde in *The Soul of Man under Socialism*, pp. 258 and 259: "Charity creates a multitude of sins" and "We are often told that the poor are grateful for charity ... but the best among the poor are never grateful. They are ungrateful, discontented, disobedient, and rebellious. They are quite right to be so." Pupils could discuss these claims in conjunction with an analysis of Mrs Birling's interrogation and as an extra point in the treatment of Additional Text 9: "The Many Aspects of Charity" (**101–102**).

Charitable institutions are not the only areas where "the ruling class" literally make the rules. They also decide what the **law** is and ultimately set, if not keep, **moral standards**. If the former is the case, it is not surprising that the older Birlings were outraged at the Inspector's behaviour. Their conclusions about the Inspector once he has left, are probably quite appropriate as a real police inspector would *not* have spoken so abruptly to them – he would have been on their side. Real police inspectors would support the Establishment and react "correctly" to the Birlings, i.e. they would do what they were told by those who run the Establishment.

This is why the question whether Goole was a real inspector, is so important for Birling and Mrs Birling. If he was a fake, the whole investigation was a fake, too. Strictly speaking the Birlings did nothing illegal, and the moral aspect is something each character must come to terms with privately. It seems as if they "have been had" and some one, "a Socialist or some sort of crank" (**74** 6–7), has succeeded in luring them out of their safe place in the social order.

Sheila and Eric see the moral question of right and wrong quite differently to their parents, and Eric's conclusion that "He was our police inspector all right" (**72** 28), shows that they have learned something about themselves and cannot go on like before. The brother and sister are affected as human beings, as individuals. They are relatively open in their attitudes, possibly because they do not run the Establishment yet – they only profit from it – and they can afford to criticize it. Whereas the brother and sister are affected as human beings, Birling and his wife retire into the **social roles** which give them their identity.

For a while, Gerald reacts like Sheila and Eric, but then he falls back into his class habits and is proud to show how one deals with such situations. Now that Goole has left, human considerations no longer matter and it is social competence that counts. Gerald may have relapsed into his old ways because being a little older, he has had more exposure to the system and he identifies more with it. He and Sheila have learned a lot about their relationship. They have both realized that although their official engagement no longer means anything, they may be able to make a new beginning as individuals.

The admission of **individual** guilt in the series of "confessions" is now seen as a sign of weakness and a betrayal of social roles. The family fight after the Inspector's departure, concentrates on who gave in most or stood up to him best. The older Birlings can return to their old position of moral authority, because now their standards are valid again.

An important indicator of the characters' social and individual roles is **language**, which in turn can reveal a great deal about the *Dramatis Personae* and their personalities. The main characteristics can be summarized as follows:

- Birling uses the pompous language of authority.
- Sheila is characterized initially by the sophisticated, witty speech of the upper-class young lady. Later however, when the occasion demands, she uses more emotional, unpretentious language.
- Eric, like Sheila, uses a lot of colloquial expressions which are natural in their age group. He is far more direct than the other characters and his language is the most uninhibited and individual of all.
- Gerald's use of language reveals him to be what he actually is, the well-educated son of wealthy, respected parents. However, he can also use quite different registers, e.g. when he talks about Meggarty, or when he talks about something that is really important to him.

Mrs Birling's attitude towards language is the most interesting of all. From the beginning, she censors her family for even minor breaches of linguistic etiquette, e.g. when Birling praises the cook after dinner. Her rigid standards however, go far beyond etiquette. For her, language organizes society according to a class code where everything has its proper place. The language she uses indicates her status and the high moral stance expected of members of the Establishment.

Mrs Birling's triumphant entry in Act II shows that she is "some one": "I'm Mrs Birling, y'know" (**38** 29), a repetition of her husband's introduction of himself in Act I. Sheila, who has been strongly influenced by the Inspector notices this at once, and begs her mother to abandon this register. The Inspector does finally force Mrs Birling to use his own direct kind of language in the scene where she comments on Eva's confession; "All a lot of nonsense – I didn't believe a word of it" and the Inspector replies; "I'm not asking you if you believed it.

I want to know what she said. Why didn't she want to take any more money from this boy?" (**58** 24–27) The Inspector does not accept her claims to a special status because if he did, the investigation would come to a standstill. It is obvious that Mrs Birling makes up her own "values" and rules and those who need help are at her mercy. She senses the rebelliousness of the young woman who has been treated badly, and therefore she regards her as a class enemy to be destroyed.

When Gerald is questioned, Mrs Birling says: "I don't think we want any further details of this disgusting affair –" (**48** 36–37), and when Gerald contradicts her with: "You know, it wasn't disgusting", she answers: "It's disgusting to me" (**49** 4–5). Exactly! For her, it is disgusting because one does not talk about such things (even if one knows they exist), whereas for Gerald it is only a question of talking honestly about his affair with Eva. Birling, too, can adopt this tone as for example when Sheila says, "But everybody knows about that horrible old Meggarty" (**45** 23–4), he imitates his socially superior wife: "*(sharply, shocked)* Sheila!" (**45** 27).

Mrs Birling's remarks about the Inspector after his departure, all concentrate on language, e.g. "Didn't I say I couldn't imagine a real police inspector talking like that to us?" (**76** 10) For once, her husband spells it out even more clearly: "Then look at the way he talked to me. Telling me to shut up – and so on. ... Besides – the way he talked – you remember. I mean, they don't *talk* like that. I've had dealings with dozens of them" (**73** 3–8). Ultimately it is not so much the facts themselves that shock the Birlings but rather that they are mentioned openly, and the language used to describe them. In their social circle, you do not say things *directly*.

Social Criticism 1912 – 1946 – 1992

Starting question: Is An Inspector Calls *a play of social criticism?*

As we have seen, the characters are all guilty to a certain degree, some possibly more than others, in that one or two of them harmed Eva directly and intentionally. Ultimately, they are faced with the choice of accepting guilt and responsibility or reclaiming their status and power.

In fact, until the Inspector opens their eyes the characters do not question their own behaviour because their upbringing and social status have conditioned them to assume that they are always right.

Initially, even Sheila does not see any injustice in being able to have a shop assistant sacked just because she happens to be angry. She reacts emotionally to this particular girl's death, but does not think critically about the whole set-up. Consequently all of the characters are types, including the young ones, despite the fact that the latter manage to free themselves from their social roles for a while.

The real scandal is that officially there is nothing wrong with their behaviour, as Birling and Mrs Birling rightly insist. In the eyes of the law they have done nothing illegal. Therefore the play focuses its criticism on the whole system, which creates a society where people are split into rigid groups and a double reality and double moral standards are accepted as the norm. Priestley shows how this society works and the effects on its members when an engagement is regarded as a business transaction: Sheila and Gerald only start to get to know each other *after* their engagement. So, the "social lie" or *Lebenslüge* (Allan Lewis, *The Contemporary Theatre*, p. 10) not only has consequences for them personally, but for society as a whole.

The implicit and explicit criticism of society in the play is supported by the tension between its different **temporal perspectives**. Taken as a play about Edwardian England, *An Inspector Calls* gives insights into a solid class society which was beginning to doubt its ideological foundations. However, this is a minor aspect which would not have created such interest in the play in 1946, of all years. For the end of the war was seen as a new beginning, the solidarity created by the war effort was to lead to a new society after the war. Eric Hobsbawm underlined this hope in *Age of Extremes,* p. 161 when he wrote, "Nobody dreamed of a postwar return to 1939 – or even to 1928 or to 1918 ... A British government under Winston Churchill committed itself, in the midst of a desperate war, to a comprehensive welfare state and full employment." Krishan Kumar comes to a similar conclusion in *The Social and Cultural Setting,* p. 16, "The war ... concentrated and consolidated ideas and movements which had been brewing in the previous decades ... As it drew to its close, it threw up the possibility of a far-reaching reconstruction of British society."

With his "Postscript" talks on the BBC during the war, Priestley had contributed a lot to these high expectations. Thus in 1946, the prophetic warnings in the Inspector's last speech took on a much more specific and urgent meaning than in the reconstructed period of 1912, in which the play was originally set. Not only had the *Titanic* sunk in the meantime, but things had to change.

Producing the Play

It is not surprising that the play was taken up by serious theatre in 1992, at a time when the country was socially divided by Thatcherite social philosophy and policies and forced to come to terms with Mrs Thatcher's denial of the very concept of society and her advocation of a return to Victorian values. This was a Britain where the Welfare State seemed on the point of collapse because of massive cuts in social spending and the British government was beginning to fight against a Social Charter in a united Europe.

The enthusiasm for a new start after the war had turned into social despair for many people and in terms of the play, the real Inspector was no longer just being announced on the phone, he was already ringing the doorbell.

Obviously, the play could not be produced like it was in 1946 and in the decades since, as if nothing had changed. A new production had to take social changes and problems, the feeling among the people and the state of contemporary society into account. So the producer transposed the message of the play into the present, and tried to visualize its meaning for contemporary Britain. The following features characterize the 1992 production of the play:

– The Birlings' living-room no longer fills the stage like a self-contained world, instead it is part of a larger world of suffering and disorder, which is already encroaching on their apparent security.

– Initially, the house towers above everything, but in the end it falls down. On stage, the inquiries take place outside the house which means that "Us" can no longer be separated from "Them" and responsibility has become public.

– The message is clear: In 1992, shutting oneself off from reality as the Birlings try to do, is even more ludicrous and irresponsible than it was in 1912, or in 1946, for that matter. This idea was taken up in many of the reviews of the play and the quote below from an article entitled "Dear Mr Priestley ..." from *Regeneration,* Winter 1994, p. 26, links the performance to the social reality awaiting the audience outside the theatre.

Well, Mr Priestley, the Labour victory you had hoped for happened, of course, and with it the establishment of the Welfare State. In the years following the war it must have seemed that we really had learnt from our mistakes and were changing for the better. But during the eighties, driven by Conservative policies, the cult of the self re-emerged with a vengeance. In 1987, three years after your death, Margaret Thatcher confidently proclaimed: "There is no such thing as society. There are individual men and women, and there are families." Full circle. You must have turned in your grave, Mr Priestley, but Stephen Daldry and the RNT have allowed your voice to be raised again in protest and pleading that we learn from the past and find hope in the younger generation.

Yours in hope,
Helen Pickering and Dom Boydell.

1) Structure

Homework: Essay Topics: 46), 48), 50), 52), 57).

The structure of the play closely follows the conventions of the three Dramatic Unities:

1. *Unity of Place*
The Birling home is the only setting.

2. *Unity of Time*
The three acts are of equal length, the division is determined by the sequence of inquiries: Act I, Birling, Sheila; Act II, Gerald, Mrs Birling; Act III, Eric. The main body of the play deals with events in the past (strictly speaking this breaks the Unity of Time although on the other hand, the past is just talked about). The structure of the play is analytical: by bringing up past events, the author provides material for the plot.

3. *Unity of Action*

The action continues without interruption throughout the work. The play starts and ends with a family scene and the middle of the play features a sequence of inquiries.

2) Plot

The plot incorporates two levels of interest, namely the inquiry into Eva's death and the Birlings' reactions, and the ensuing family quarrels. Admittedly, the plot is somewhat contrived as it is highly improbable that all of the characters would have been involved with Eva. On top of this, the plot is worked out rather mechanically as the characters are questioned one by one.

On the other hand, Priestley manages to achieve great variety within the play as each character is involved in a very individual way and reacts very differently to both his/her own actions and to those of the other characters. As the inquiries proceed, the characters take more active roles in finding out the truth, and they also take sides. In this way, the family storyline breaks up the potential monotony of the plot structure.

3) Suspense

The contrived nature of the plot is broken up by suspense in a number of ways as the latter is naturally kept up by the court-room atmosphere of the individual interrogations. The outcome of the inquiries is not predictable in that the questioning procedure constantly changes direction, moving between the typical thriller approaches of Who? What? How? etc.

The arrangement of **Exits** and **Entrances** heightens the suspense. Mrs Birling's re-entrance in Act II, for example, is made more spectacular by virtue of her ignorance of events since the Inspector's arrival. The other characters and the audience are a step ahead of her, which makes her hubris and subsequent downfall more dramatic.

4) Dramatic Irony

One of the most important elements in the play, dramatic irony, is used on various levels.

a) Ironic tension is produced by the knowledge that despite the solid facade, the world of 1912 was soon to be completely destroyed.

Birling's reference to the Titanic as being "absolutely unsinkable" (**12** 13), is loaded with connotations for a modern audience: "The Titanic is the most enduring modern image of disaster." (Terry Coleman, *Thatcher's Britain*, p. 157). In his book, Coleman compiled a whole list of political allusions to the Titanic disaster, ranging from the Watergate affair in 1973, to the British election campaign of 1987 when David Steel, the chairman of the Liberal-Democratic Alliance, said that "if Mrs Thatcher had been captain of the Titanic she would have reassured passengers that the ship had only stopped to take on ice."

b) From the beginning, Priestley uses "pointers" based on situational irony, i.e. statements by characters which later turn out to be the opposite of the truth:

- "You seem to be a nice well-behaved family – " (**14** 15–16).
- "Unless Eric has been up to something" (**17** 1–2).
- "It's a perfectly straightforward case" (**20** 28–29).
- "You talk as if we were responsible" (**26** 18–19).
- "I don't think we can help you much" (**38** 32–33).

c) In the stricter sense of the term, situational irony is employed "by the members of the audience who have been apprised of a character's real situation before he knows it himself, and who can therefore anticipate and enjoy the frustration of the ideal by the actual" (Roger Fowler, ed. *A Dictionary of Modern Critical Terms*, p. 101).

Mrs Birling's hubris in Act II provides the best example of this, because at that moment she is the very embodiment of "Birlingism". The impact is only softened because there are no real, "official" consequences for the Birlings.

d) At one point, the Inspector spells out the pervading irony of the play when he counters Gerald's differentiation between "respectable citizens" and "criminals" with: "Sometimes there isn't as much difference as you think. Often, if it was left to me, I wouldn't know where to draw the line" (**30** 31–33).

Post-reading Activities

1) Imagine Acts IV and V: A **Real** Inspector Calls.

2) a) "Gerald: Yes, I know what you mean. But I'm coming back – if I may.
Sheila: All right" (**51** 12–14).

b) "Gerald: Everything's all right now, Sheila ... What about this ring?
Sheila: No, not yet. It's too soon. I must think" (**86** 37–**87** 1).

Do Sheila and Gerald have a future together? Try to imagine a "new" relationship.

3) If the play were placed in a contemporary setting, which elements would be different? Consider the following key words:

Strikes: Workers generally have more freedom nowadays, including some degree of job security and the right to strike.

Job Security (Eva at Milwards): This depends very much on legal formalities (type of contract, tenure, specified working conditions). It's highly unlikely, although not impossible that the scene at Milwards could happen nowadays.

Charity: The welfare state has, to a large extent, taken over from charities which means that Eva would get a maternity allowance, even if she was single or unemployed. Eric would be required to pay maintenance for the child. Pupils should cross-reference Top Line, *Chapter 3, "Modern Britain", and the "Fact File" particularly on Thatcherism, p. 288 f.*

Morality: This point is obviously much more difficult to discuss because it is hard to assess how binding moral standards are in our society nowadays.

Working with the Additional Texts

The additional texts have been specially selected to link up with the themes of the play and can be dealt with either after or while the play is being read. This approach helps to broaden discussions and leads away from purely literary aspects. The following classification may be helpful in deciding which of the texts can be used together:

1) Social background – texts 2, 8, and 10.
2) Social contrasts and working conditions – texts 3, 4, 5 and 6.
3) Society, class and charity – texts 7 and 9.
4) Reviews – texts 12 and 13.
5) Literature and society – texts 1, 11, and 14.

1. John Boynton Priestley: A Chronology
11. Priestley, the Man and the Playwright

Pupils should refer to Additional Text: 1 in order to fill in the details of Priestley's life and work which Burgess refers to in his assessment of the author. Indeed the first sentence of Burgess's review sums up Priestley as a "demotic communicator". The key to his popularity and the accessibility of his works may lie in the answer Priestley gave to a criticism that his writing was "too simple": "But I've spent years and years trying to make my writing simple. What you see as a fault, I regard as a virtue." (*Too Simple?* from *Delight*, in: *The Priestley Companion: Extracts from the Writings of J. B. Priestley Selected by Himself*, p. 404 ff.)

1) What is meant by "the niceties of art"? (l. 3) Think of what is considered "modern" in modern literature.
2) Can you detect any "formal quirkiness" and "decently diluted intellectuality" (l. 22) in the play?
3) What does "he avoided pretension" (ll. 22–23) mean in literary terms?
4) What does the claim "what he humbly did he humbly did well" (ll. 23–24) mean exactly? Would you describe Priestley's style as being "humble"?
5) What kind of writer was Priestley? List the literary genres he tried his hand at.
6) Find copies and translations of Priestley's works in your local library. (Priestley's novels are very readable and suitable for book reports.)

7) List Priestley's non-literary activities and find out more about them.
8) a) Priestley has often been called a "committed writer". Illustrate this point using his biography for reference.
b) Do you think a writer should be committed? In what way? Link the ideas put forward in Additional Text: 14 with the discussion of Priestley's commitment as a writer.

2. A Pleasure Ground for the Rich

The text describes the two sides of Edwardian Britain. One side is illustrated by key words like contrasts, inequalities, social reform, guilt, poverty and protest. Key words like "Golden Age" suggest a more nostalgic view of Edwardian Britain. The contrast is summed up with the phrases, "pleasure ground for the rich"/"treasure house for the nation" (ll. 11–12). In fact, Edwardian Britain was the richest country in the world and Queen Victoria's Diamond Jubilee in 1897 marked the climax of British imperial power.

The double image of Edwardian Britain is a standard feature of British historiography. In *England in the Twentieth Century* (p. 15f.), David Thomson describes the feeling in 1919 when people looked back on the prewar days "as a golden age of stability and prosperity, a civilization to be as far as possible recaptured and restored save for those few flaws which, they believed, had led to the disaster of general war."

1) Why did Priestley choose Edwardian Britain as a setting for his play?
2) Which elements in the text are reflected in the play's characters and setting?

3. Masters and Servants

This text provides hard facts about the distribution of wealth in Edwardian Britain (strictly speaking, Edwardian Britain ended in 1910, but the label is generally used to cover the years up to World War I as well). It can be discussed as an outside commentary, after the opening scene, or after Birling has been questioned.

1) Find direct points of contact with the play in the first paragraph of the text.

2) Pupils could work out the percentage of income that went towards paying staff and compare this to salaries nowadays.

For example, a housemaid earning £16 a year from her employer, a lawyer, who earns £600 a year, receives 2.5% of his income. By applying this percentage to a modern salary, e.g. 5,000 units a month, a full-time housemaid without fixed working-hours and often without a day off, without extra costs for health insurance, pension, unemployment insurance, etc. would earn 125 units. She would, of course, get board and lodging of a kind, i.e. she would eat with the other domestic staff, and sleep in the kitchen, a box-room or a room in the cellar. For comparison purposes, pupils should find out how much a cleaner in a private house earns.

Then they could work out the other figures in the text in a similar way, to get an idea of how big the gap between rich and poor was. Even industrial wages were no better than those received in domestic service. In the "liberal" economy of the day, workers were at the mercy of the employers who regarded the distribution of wealth described in the text, as normal.

4. Working Conditions

This excerpt from Gissing's *The Odd Women* throws light on conditions for Eva at Milwards and can be introduced after Sheila has been questioned.

1) What kind of character is Rhoda Nunn?
2) Comment on her use of irony.
3) What is her strategy for solving the problems described by Monica?
4) Does she really believe in this strategy?
5) What is Monica's role in this scene?
6) Sum up Monica's working conditions.

5. The Labour Market

This text relates directly to Eva as a worker and in particular to her time at the Birling works. It is suitable for discussion after the Inspector has exposed Birling's role as an employer in Act I.

1) What kind of industrial society does Shaw describe?
   (Classical "liberal" economy where everything is left to the market forces dependent on the supply and demand of labour. There are no commonly accepted or legally enforced standards to regulate this mechanism, e.g. minimum wage, laws regulating working conditions, etc.)
2) What does he mean by "thoughtful" and "public spirited" (ll. 13, 18)?
3) What, in Shaw's view, is the role of the government?
4) What do you think is meant by "the barest limits of common humanity" (ll. 29–30)?
5) How does Shaw see the roles of employers and workers? Does he take sides?
6) Discuss how labour relations and unions, collective bargaining, social and job security, the welfare state, etc. have changed since the text was written in the late twenties. Use your Systematic Vocabulary to find the words you need.

6. The Justice of the Peace
Cp. Pre-Reading Activities, p. 8–10 of this *Guide*.

7. Them and Us

The concept of "Them and Us" is obviously central to the play and to the Birlings' social philosophy (cp. especially Birling's and Goole's speeches). Shaw's expository text outlines theses which are developed in the course of the play. The text can be discussed after Mrs Birling's scene, or once pupils have read the play and the overall problems have come into perspective.

This notion of "Them and Us" has not only been employed in tbe Social Debate in postwar Britain to describe social alienation and class differences, but also as a source of working-class solidarity, notably in Richard Hoggart's epoch-making book *The Uses of Literacy* (first 1957) p. 53. Hoggart puts forward the theory that "most groups gain some of their strength from their exclusiveness, from a sense of people outside who are not 'Us'." 'Them' however includes all those who have official jobs or enjoy positions of power. He rounds off this notion with "To the very poor, especially, they compose a shadowy but numerous and powerful group affecting their lives at almost every point: the world is divided into 'Them' and 'Us'." Obviously it is not just the members of the upper class who feel that this division of society is justified but also those unfortunate enough to be in the so-called lower classes.

1. a) Could the concept of "Them and Us" be used to describe structures in your society?

   b) If so, who would take on the roles of "Them" and "Us"?

8. Changes in Social Structures after 1945

The text which was taken from *British Society since 1945* by Arthur Marwick, illustrates the upheaval and the social climate in postwar Britain when *An Inspector Calls* was first produced. These factors and the memory of the years before the war meant that the audience were more receptive to the message of the play. The 1992 production, on the other hand, takes the reactionary tendencies of the Thatcher years into account.

Pupils could deal with this text in conjunction with Additional Text: 10, looking in particular at how the social climate of the day influences the audience, its expectations and reactions, and thereby affects the message of a play like *An Inspector Calls*. It would also be appropriate to refer back to the short excerpts from Hobsbawm and Kumar, p. 36 of this *Guide*.

1. Try to reconstruct the frame of mind of theatregoers in 1946 and again in 1992.
2. "The message of a play is always affected by the social conditions the audience live in." Discuss.

9. The Many Aspects of Charity

At first glance, charity is always a good thing, but Williams shows the complex nature of charity in any social system: Private charity is based on ideologies of some kind and is always dependent on the goodwill of individuals or groups who grant it. This aspect of the text helps both to define Mrs Birling's idea of charity more clearly and to put it into a historical perspective. The text also outlines how, in the public domain, charity is seen as a human right and is distributed as part of a welfare system. This idea is taken a step further in Additional Text: 10. "The Homeless in Contemporary Britain" when Anthony Sampson looks at what happens when the social services, which took over the role of charity, themselves are cut back. In the context of the play, the Birlings get Eva into trouble, and then the same Birlings are supposed to help her. The motives and underlying assumptions of the Birlings are the same throughout and are based on the concept of "Them and Us".

A further reference for this topic is Brecht's *Die Nachtlager* which pupils could discuss in English. This poem shows the dialectical nature of charity: Charity helps those who need it, in this case a bed is offered for the night, but this does not change the reasons for homelessness, namely the underlying social system, and we can say that charity actually perpetuates this system.

1. Does a comprehensive social network make charity unnecessary nowadays?

10. The Homeless in Contemporary Britain

This text links up directly with a very noticeable aspect of the new poverty in Britain mentioned in many reviews of Daldry's 1992 production. Pupils could also refer to Additional Text: 13.

1) Why are so many people homeless?
2) Why can the Welfare State not cope with this problem?
3) How would you explain the fact that so many dwellings are empty while half a million people are homeless?

11. Priestley, the Man and the Playwright

Cp. Additional Text: 1, pp. 42–43 of this *Guide*.

12. Stage Production – 1946. A Review

1) Which aspects of the play does the reviewer concentrate on?
2) What does he mean by "theatrical ethics" (l. 4)?
3) Is *An Inspector Calls* a "moralising play" (l. 4)?
4) What exactly is the "fatal dead-end" he criticizes in l. 11? Do you agree with his criticism?

5) According to the reviewer, why is the play put "into an Edwardian scene and costume"(ll. 18–19)? Do you agree with his reasoning?
6) In your view, is this a good review? What is a good review?

13. Stage Production – 1994. A Review

1) Which aspects of the play does the review concentrate on?
2) Comment on ll. 1–2 and 37–38: Why does the critic think Lady Thatcher should see the play?
3) "Picking our way over the homeless in the Strand on our way home tonight will be more than usually tricky" (ll. 12–13). Explain and comment.
4) Do you think this is a good review? Give reasons.
5) Compare the two reviews.

14. The Theatre as a Political Forum

This text can be discussed either as part of the Pre-Reading Activities, or after the play has been read, together with Additional Texts: 1 and 11, under the heading "Literature, Drama and Society".

Obviously, McGrath's ideas aim at what could be broady termed as political theatre, and this puts him in a line with Brecht, Piscator, and Rolf Hochhuth. This line is clearly opposed to mainstream drama in Britain, where theatre subsidies are low and commercial theatres often have to use any means to attract audiences. Priestley is less dogmatic about the function of the theatre, but for him, too, it is "one of the few common meeting places ... Where there is self-consciousness, there – you may say – the Theatre has set up its platform and curtains." (*Why the Theatre?* from *Midnight in the Desert* in: *The Priestley Companion: Extracts from the Writings of J. B. Priestley Selected by Himself,* p. 401ff).

It is interesting that political drama is having a comeback in Britain, e.g. David Hare's immensely successful trilogy *Racing Demon* (1990), *Murmuring Judges* (1991) and *The Absence of War* (1993) which deals with the Church, the Law, and modern politicians and politics, respectively, and the accompanying volume *Asking Around. Background to the David Hare Trilogy* (1993) which constitutes a social studies handbook of contemporary Britain.

1) Sum up, in your own words, what McGrath sees as the function of the theatre in society.
2) Do you think this is how most theatregoers see theatre? What do people expect from a "good night out" at the theatre?
3) Are these different expectations mutually exclusive?
4) What do you expect from a play? What kind of plays do you like?
5) Write a review of a play you have seen recently.

Suggested Test: I

The following excerpt is from Act I of *An Inspector Calls* (**13** 20–**14** 28).
Read the text carefully, then complete the tasks.

BIRLING	Thanks. *(Confidentially)* By the way, there's something I'd like to mention – in strict confidence – while we're by ourselves. I have an idea that your mother – Lady Croft – while she doesn't object to my girl – feels you might have done better for yourself socially –

(Gerald, rather embarrassed, begins to murmur some dissent, but Birling checks him.)

	No, Gerald, that's all right. Don't blame her. She comes from an old county family – landed people and so forth – and so it's only natural. But what I wanted to say is – there's a fair chance that I might find my way into the next Honours List. Just a knighthood, of course.
GERALD	Oh – I say – congratulations!
BIRLING	Thanks. But it's a bit too early for that. So don't say anything. But I've had a hint or two. You see, I was Lord Mayor here two years ago when Royalty visited us. And I've always been regarded as a sound useful party man. So – well – I gather there's a very good chance of a knighthood – so long as we behave ourselves, don't get into the police court or start a scandal – eh? *(Laughs complacently.)*
GERALD	*(laughs)* You seem to be a nice well-behaved family –
BIRLING	We think we are –
GERALD	So if that's the only obstacle, sir, I think you might as well accept my congratulations now.
BIRLING	No, no, I couldn't do that. And don't say anything yet.
GERALD	Not even to my mother? I know she'd be delighted.
BIRLING	Well, when she comes back, you might drop a hint to her. And you can promise her that we'll try to keep out of trouble during the next few months.

Reprinted by permission of the Peters Fraser & Dunlop Group Ltd.

I. Vocabulary

Explain the following words within the given context:
a) line 1:   *confidentially*
b) line 4:   *to object*
c) line 8:   *dissent*
d) line 8:   *to check*
e) line 12:   *fair*
f) lines 13–14: *just a knighthood*
g) line 18:   *Royalty*
h) line 20:   *sound*
i) line 20:   *to gather*

II. Comprehension

Answer the following questions using complete sentences.
1. Place this scene in the dramatic context of Act I.
2. What is the scene about? What does it tell us about Birling?
3. There are several "pointers" in this scene, i.e. remarks which become important in the course of the play. Find and discuss them.
4. Study the auctorial comments in brackets. In what way do they help you to understand the scene better?

III. Essay

Gerald.

Suggested Test: II

The following excerpt is from Act I of *An Inspector Calls* (**32** 12–**33** 12).
Read the text carefully, then complete the tasks.

SHEILA   I'd gone in to try something on. It was an idea of
my own – mother had been against it, and so had
the assistant – but I insisted. As soon as I tried it
on, I knew they'd been right. It just didn't suit me
5   at all. I looked silly in the thing. Well, this girl had
brought the dress up from the workroom, and
when the assistant – Miss Francis – had asked her
something about it, this girl, to show us what she
meant, had held the dress up, as if she was wearing
10   it. And it just suited her. She was the right type for
it, just as I was the wrong type. She was a very
pretty girl too – with big dark eyes – and that didn't
make it any better. Well, when I tried the thing on
and looked at myself and knew that it was all
15   wrong, I caught sight of this girl smiling at Miss
Francis – as if to say: 'Doesn't she look awful' –
and I was absolutely furious. I was very rude to
both of them, and then I went to the manager and
told him that this girl had been very impertinent –
20   and – and – *(She almost breaks down, but just*
controls herself.) How could I know what would
happen afterwards? If she'd been some miserable
plain little creature, I don't suppose, I'd have done
it. But she was very pretty and looked as if she
25   could take care of herself. I couldn't be sorry for her.
INSPECTOR   In fact, in a kind of way, you might be said to have
been jealous of her.
SHEILA   Yes, I suppose so.
INSPECTOR   And so you used the power you had, as a daughter
30   of a good customer and also of a man well-known
in the town, to punish the girl just because she
made you feel like that?
SHEILA   Yes, but it didn't seem to be anything very terrible
at the time. Don't you understand? And if I could
35   help her now, I would –

Reprinted by permission of the Peters Fraser & Dunlop Group Ltd.

I. Comprehension

1. Place this scene in the dramatic context of Act I.
2. Compare Sheila's reaction, when she realizes what she has done, to Birling's reaction, in the scene before.

II. Translation

Translate ll. 1–20 into German.

III. Creative Writing

Write a dialogue between the manager of Milwards and Eva Smith, after Sheila has complained about her. Remember what type of person Eva is, and imagine the awkward situation the manager is in. You might start like this:

MANAGER: Now, Miss Smith, Miss Birling – you know Miss Birling, of course – has just complained about you. I don't need to tell you this is a very serious matter. What exactly happened?

EVA: ...

Bibliography

Braine, John: *J. B. Priestley*. London: Weidenfeld and Nicholson, 1978.

Briggs, Asa: *A Social History of England*. London: Penguin, 1987².

Coleman, Terry: *Thatcher's Britain*. London: Corgi Books, 1988².

Fowler, Roger ed.: *A Dictionary of Modern Critical Terms*. London: Routledge & Kegan Paul, 1973.

Gray, Katie: *J. B. Priestley, An Inspector Calls. York Notes*. London: Longman York Press, 1994⁸.

Hampton, Christopher ed.: *A Radical Reader. The Struggle for Change in England, 1381–1914*. London: Penguin, 1984.

Hare, David: *Asking Around. Background to the David Hare Trilogy*, London: faber and faber, 1993.

Hare, David: *Murmuring Judges*, London: faber and faber, 1991.

Hare, David: *Racing Demon*, London: faber and faber, 1990.

Hare, David: *The Absence of War*, London: faber and faber, 1993.

Harris, Jose: *Private Lives, Public Spirit: Britain 1870–1914*. London: Penguin, 1993.

Hobsbawm, Eric: *Age of Extremes. The Short Twentieth Century 1914–1991*. London: Michael Joseph, 1994.

Hoggart, Richard: *The Uses of Literacy*. London: Penguin, 1959.

Klein, Holger: *J. B. Priestley's Plays*. London: Macmillan, 1988.

Kumar, Krishan: *The Social and Cultural Setting*, in: *The New Pelican Guide to English Literature*, ed. Boris Ford, *Vol. 8: The Present*. London: Penguin, 1983.

Lewis, Allan: *The Contemporary Theatre*. New York: Crown, 1962.

Martin, Stewart: *J. B. Priestley, An Inspector Calls. Letts Literature Guides*. London: Letts Educational Ltd., 1994.

Marwick, Arthur: *British Society since 1945*. London: Penguin, 1982.

McGrath, John: *A Good Night Out*. London: Eyre Methuen, 1981.

Peinert, Dietrich: *J. B. Priestley, An Inspector Calls. Praxis des neusprachlichen Unterrichts*, 13/4, 1966.

Priestley, J. B.: *An Inspector Calls. Theatre Programme*. Aldwych Theatre, London, 1993 (about Stephen Daldry's production).

Priestley, J. B.: *The Priestley Companion. Extracts from the Writings of J. B. Priestley Selected by Himself*. London: Penguin, 1951.

Ruddock, Joan: *CND Scrapbook*. London: Optima Books, Macdonald & Co., 1987.

Sampson, Anthony: *The Essential Anatomy of Britain*. London: Hodder & Stoughton, 1992.

Shaw, Bernard: *The Intelligent Woman's Guide to Socialism, Capitalism, Sovietism and Fascism*. London: Penguin, 1965.

Stevenson, John: *British Society 1914–45*, London: Penguin, 1984.

Thomson, David: *England in the Twentieth Century*, London: Penguin, 1965.

Wilde, Oscar: *The Soul of Man under Socialism*, in: *O. W., Plays, Prose Writings and Poems*. London: Dent & Sons, Everyman Paperbacks, 1960.

Williams, Raymond: *The Social History of Dramatic Forms*, in: *The Long Revolution*. London: Penguin, 1965.

Williams, Raymond: *Drama in Performance*. London: Penguin, 1968.

Williams, Raymond: *Keywords*. London: Fontana, 1976.

Young, Kenneth: *J. B. Priestley*. London: Longman Ltd. for the British Council, 1977 (Writers and Their Work 257).